PARADES

PARADES

Sara Deniz Akant

Cover photo by the author

Cover and interior design by Peter Burghardt

Typefaces: Albertus MT Standard and Garamond Premier Pro

Offset printed in the United States
by Edwards Brothers Malloy, Ann Arbor, Michigan
On 55# Enviro Natural 100% Recycled 100% PCW
Acid Free Archival Quality FSC Certified Paper
with Rainbow FSC Certified Colored End Papers

Published by Omnidawn Publishing, Richmond, California
www.omnidawn.com   (510) 237-5472   (800) 792-4957
10 9 8 7 6 5 4 3 2 1
ISBN: 978-1-890650-75-9

CONTENTS

THE SHIP

go we here or [sleep
by sleep] our ship
unless we go

the rattled ghost [you're in it
in the yoke] without
the bone

go restless as we bathe
and stretch [at last]
that I may feel

miles six
six hungers in our ship
[or hollow home]

so now we go lest
rest by rest [we
sink] unless
we go

THE KINGDOM

--- ---- ----- ------ ------- -------- --------- ---------- ----------

ancient gamma
once theirs to lay
shrouded in oh no the centuries
that left her here. to doctors
who stray in this perfect loop
they glare. for even to shake
with perhaps her dress has
perhaps gone once
and gone out of
the spiritual.

[con ono vis ospit
er gamma moo say
her loo blie dogon
her keith bliar fock]

a frock : the fur of tiny living
and
the moose : of our open
escaping.

[to der stool ella
glay fer ley
a dig blie innig
fer dat kampling vay]

--- ---- ----- ------ ------- -------- --------- ---------- ----------

THE KINGDOM

--- ---- ----- ------ ------- -------- --------- ---------- ----------

who can lay in the ghost stays old. say no. say
a longer beyond may be possible.

and twins get cold with animal things.
so fuse us not. we are unique.

one face exposes miles.
say ash is to ashes and uncoupled dust.

these sleeping islands.
they'll give the pitch.

one beat is cross one
song is acid one
horse is running
its distance lost.

--- ---- ----- ------ ------- -------- --------- ---------- ---------

THE KINGDOM

--- ---- ----- ------ ------- -------- --------- ---------- ----------

it was a life coming up from a gap in the floor. it came up a twisted
and quiet. then backed itself down. and she thought my self against
something is emptying me into the room. but take me through
the motions. what do you think is
my face is for.

the light that got through the mask hit her forehead. burning the holes just
above her eyelids. now things moved out and not into
all the right places. it made the desire for scratching. for
having tongues at the tips of the fingers in the place
of the nail with razor sharp edges that could
rip through the seams and take all the
foreign bodies out.

                              I would never

she kept telling herself over and over
I would never throw away
the core.

the place it took place in was like
an alpine tree.
a very precise ratio of surface to speed.
the desire for an entry. [con ono :
vis ospit]

--- ---- ----- ------ ------- -------- --------- ---------- ----------

OPERATION GINGER

saying it gingerly, say
the hall is a disaster
is an integral part of the hall. say
how are we going to tank on tank in
to it softly, going softly for Ginger, go
in howling for Ginger, for Ginger is
here. and I have no time for she.

OPERATION GINGER
[second report]

with an occasional vortex,   Ginger feels the plexiglass in
slow waves. from moment-to-moment,   this is a period of
zero time. of silence, and so forth.

but she was frightened   to see the rays of light
as they drifted from the micro-objects.   she questioned
the specific meaning of darkness, and so forth.

this led her into things   with a greater sensitivity
than the digital subtest had predicted.

with no direct concern   for deep sleep bodies
the spontaneous tone   studies Ginger as its subject.

it drops in   on her basal skin responses
with the door open   and so forth

GEORGIA

Georgia is deep with the weather tonight. surrounded goes
through it, she is helpless but reefing. the men in the
basement were talking in floorboards. she tacked up to
marshland and charged for the air.

> now they are there and now they are not.
> sno iva la denté, sno ivé denog.

what matters is she has bad hands for this stuff. will pick up
on dryness in the fall of the month. when the storm had a
value, she built shores in its flight. when the dunes slid to
Georgia, the ocean had light.

> where did it happen? derento de bonnist.
> when was avatron? haven't the foggiest.
> why kliné de lobe? bons latta, la gait.
> to der ellé vontronten? on the stairs.
> she was late.

on static severe, Georgia sank in her flowers. the polyhedron
shapes Georgia, going damp for her stillness. she memorized
in sand links but forgot how to find them. ripping tones
through the hallway, her windows in fog.

what a constant to dailoft, de levanté
the walls. if there is light hara innig,
horta brink that was sought. the way
seemed too narrow, satoro, to open.
she slept through the breakers, hyne
limpé, limpog.

what matters is she has bad hands for this weather. packed
water for days, wrote up notes in her chest. the dark forms
made shadows before their motions could start. there are
souls in the basement drifting Georgia apart.

dela heavenly host in dehyde have none
hacka no moosen, Georgia minsé run.

°∫°   °∫°

°∫°

°∫°

COLOPHON, IF THERE EVER WAS ONE
stiff larva on these ports. flat shadows flaunting, pictures?
and the rock that boundless, floats.

°∫°

INHALT: A DIRE BOAT
some fancy napkins and a hammer : what good could
such things do. living on our tempered flags, the blood-
black wonder, glued.

°∫°

ESCAPE THE VIOLETE MOON
there was a war, in any case, our sister moved upstairs.
she stood six strokes from bank to bank, cut four pieces
from her hair.

°∫°

OUR ACTRESS SMELLS THE SECRET LAIR
so wistful, plastic figures! one face that eight lines drew. smile
midnight shores and glance-out : build a flood to rendezvous.

°∫°

°∫°

°∫°

°∫°

STILLE HOUSE WITHOUT THE TUNE
oh, what manic purple shrubs! such space must fade out
hunger, as our fixed arms dance above.

°∫°

THE BOY-O-BOY FAÇADE
the empty yards ran close to channel, dawned less the less
she moved. from now on we light pallid organs, go the darker
into woods.

°∫°

A PATTERN SPECTRE STOOD
but we could never brace the waves that sang our sister's
tune. strange trees, she cried, and feigned a frown, strange
trees that still wont bloom.

°∫°

HOTELS THAT MASKE THE ROOM
and when we tried to smooth her face, she drifted through
the dune.

°∫°

°∫°

°∫°   °∫°

APRIL LTD.

_/[-]_

who woke tolante thimbles just to
skelesuck the dawn. all fired into
scarlet, carved up face "obilatron." had
blossoms tumbled sorgust, one nature
lump, two-beat. still scorching holtige
in and out to light her purple beach.

who can sleep a major? hodovars of the grave.
what vinlox sinks the minor? some lonefut, riglet. stay.

the slogang slips away. but April sculpts the balogun
and nohtos the escape.

the upshot is that, far from skartt,
she capes and lopes the storm.
interlacing straps to figure, April twists
then mirrors on. half- nailed to,
"ogata!" what timpired up the tape.
eight infants with four bloompa. eight
times no less fearsome eight.

bare sintas, untuned. where to echo the yoke when to empty the
dune. why follow the famma, sic'lic, the mono-moon.

what dirroda lurks, "irriki!"
who slopes April's slopes too soon.

ITGARA 2.0

{" ~ "}
(/(/)

we saved before the showing [*lakisma*] could detect her. two years in which we think to, and we imagined she was so. we did the *la'lick* backwards, scrubbed off [*dustan*] for her roots. worked out much we now admit to, and she would soon possess the glue.

her poshlin, common error, made us famous long ago. different *dromlics* work the humans [just the ones who work at home]. simple snooping makes them *kanyas* [gentle fixed winds] : how they blow. blow her famous in traversing, sail necessary, slow.

the detainment block [*larayna*] becomes her arbitrary glow. and this beds us in yumcaya, sends us deeper *forsimo*. her fame while yet traversing has reached open season show. savage hands that still have trend rights, still conceive her as she goes. her cycling gone nearer [*rik'lik*] gone nearer, to the place with [*ic*] the flowers.

UPTRON

[-"_"-]
/|\

even so it wasn't, the closer, in thicket. he looked the
case over, for spalicht, a flicker. the face did no witness.
there were holes through the jaw. its micro-lace pattern
would not open too far.

"malatra von nada," spun dense lawn, *voila*
one *pitlore*, sans limber, "fulfilling the thaw"

even so it wasn't, there were differences throughout. for
example, *sitoomba*, which stood pink from the start. in
any case it wasnt, for Uptron, too late. the yard he
inspected sank miles. two lakes.

two lakes of the *timbron* three lakes for the rot
four lakes in a weakness but none *tassletoft*

he sought forest madness, what Uptron had sought.
a simpler bandit would just rip his mask off.

^ WILBASO ^

^ half-trolling ^ the eies they ^ have
^ comp they web ^ our day

half-dump ^ ish ^ at
toncé ^ half-gloam
in ^ wico
lade ^

so gladsome in this nest ^
^ so ^ riptron ^ thal
amus ^ that lode
stone ^ gator

etched ^

dense passing, what orbits, and still our
polar rot. slick land of the dark
pools, what whispers may patch up.
these holes have secret plugsong :
what travels narrow ways. there was
never much to question.
it is coming. it is great.

to be sure, what sent out sinlore ———— stenched the decades that collide.
drawing nearer into solid, what the waves could ———————— sensitize. ———
———————— interlace this roaring center, cold straps could —————————
build a room. tugging necessary, tender —————————————————————
—————————————————————————— what moves darkling to the dune.

this thicket throbs the marshland, what
pinks in morning yards. the mouth
had nothing nearer than the grass : a
ruthless thaw. inspect our patterns
brightly, step cold, the afternoon.
flicker eight to sever eighty.
there are eighty-seven rooms.

what made out simple fields ---------- and you have to wonder why.
--- which is to say --- what shouldered ---- when in mass was meant
to fly. ---- what stubbornly persisted verged on --- tearing up the wall.
--------------------------- some eyes snapped rooms to figure
---------------------- floating groundless, soft to fall. --------

∞ ∞ ∞

no save, no show. by the roots of some
procession. what works against the
pitfront, fix damp in it our homes.
microfigures of the centaur burst the
famous onto shores. no flowers near
this lake and now the nothing
spins below.

graves, what vague mechanic graves. ─────────────────────────
nothing in those thirty seconds ────── could have possibly been saved.
────────────── sweeping snouts, what strengths beyond this station.
──── one yellow, one orange ──────────────────────────────
─────────── stood the violent gray location. ─────────────────

as for Trant, he travels alone. regarded
rather stilton in the field. so now we
count upon the closure. we count upon
the Cathedral. we count upon the ones
who build the morning : hustle, kneel.

.

.

it was odd. it was a halo of white hair.
a halo of white hair that followed Stilton
through the field.

.

.

.

.

.

.

stone, storm, Stilton, animal. still morning,
one might say.

.

.

so now we trot, trot. we trant,
trant. he is a small,
brown. he is Stilton and he digs.

‾ICROLO ‾

neese to look ‾out
at ‾eies to look up ‾in

the necessary feel ‾
‾in the ‾diso

plino ‾

‾morn

-

-

-

-

THE ICERUNG

.

.

.

she wade through
the icerung. he had
been in two
minds. in the
continental habit
of even, clean
churches.

> her inné : der stuté
> ein stad skin sol.

.

.

.

her shortest rib is
one such. with
or without, it is his
only bow to live by.
> on lievré, on vraho,
> sonatin : pools.

.

.

.

.
.
.

have you forgotten the
condol [on tomadé de
eisrung] have you a stop
on the ponder, the slow
melda, tyne?

be aware that he was there :
hip-bone dropped in silence.

MARK

for a darkness does not lift no ------------
other vessel. ----------------------------------

for a tunnel of itself does less ---------- in
grinding less ------------------------ to sink
the grounds of ---------------------------- no
less wall. --------------------------------------

against the scratching of --------------------
---------------------------- his ancient spring.

---------------------------- sink digestion vs.
-------------------------------------- grinding.
he kept as even as ----------------------------
if springing out -------------------- the even
------------------------------ scratching wall.

the thickest horse flung open of ------------------ itself the
-- very vessel.
a sink of all who lay there etched the -----

---------- mark that kept the pace. ---------

------------------------------- oh Mark who kept the most
------------------------------- part kept the spring he kept
the pace --------------------

ASTRID

in spring at last -------- the slowly sketches stalked
the unmarked wall. so still past through the room.
and was this not ------------------------- her long-lost
pool? -------------------------------- for all departures
call revival. ------------------------------------- to simple
ground that slowly is ------------------------------------

------------------------- the astrid -----------------------
------------------------- of the hall -----------------------

oh Astrid of the hall -------------------------------------
who falls -------------- to glances of that ------- pose.
------------ to dwell in lung straight wings to stretch
the action of the swell. -----------------------------------
------------------ she splonded through ----------------
--------- she splonded through -------------------------
--------- to halt ---
at no less wall. ---
------------------------- the silence white and absolute

----------------------- of all the ways --------------------
----------------------- to pace her there -----------------

THE BABOON

since each of us was several,   we went as
even as we dared.   it was   our *magnum opus*,
the capture of   a code.   or was it
something else entirely : the host, or

                                                         the baboon?
I say there is another puppet.   I say it forms its own cocoon.

since each of us was several,   we went to
something else entirely,   the couchgrass
even as we dared. it   was our.   *magna focus* :
the capture of a   code.   or was it for

                                                           the moon.
I say there is another puppet.   who forms this roaring, roaring tune?

since each of us was several,   we went for
the capture of a code.   it was as
even as we dared. it was   our *mondiopus*, or
something else entirely : the organ

                                                       and the loom.
I say there is another puppet   who forms a type of? sort of tomb.

the capture of a code...   was it? or
something else entirely, the sound as
even as we dared.   it was our *magni locus*,
                                                     an open-ended wound.
                                                     we went. but still :
since each of us was several,
I say there is another puppet   who forms a private *nom-de-plume*.

since each of us was several,   we went in
even as we dared.   was it   our *magnum opus*,
the capture of   a code?   no : it was
something else entirely   an organ in

                                                              the dune.
I say there is another puppet.   I say it forms its own cocoon.

                    in several forms, our magnum *swoons. even puppets as
                    we dared. I am the host. I say that each
                    of us was several. but still, because of
                    the baboon*

                                                                    .

                                                                    .

                                                                    .

                                                                    .

THE DESCENDANT

we counted on the crossbills, for hours, on
end. long before the text had fallen, it had
bordered on the grounds. black larches, those
jackdaws, lets assemble such avengers. in this
scheme, all the while, we are working one-to-one.

in this scheme, all the while, had we any hope
for a descendant. paved the way for squirrels
and organs, the final stages of such fade. the more
[or less : the almost] of those who still, traversing.
as history recounts that, at the center of this mound.

at the center of this mound, this world will touch
with others. fast away inside a pillow, the outer
stages of such flight. some bits of lint to ripen, one
distinguished from the rest. massed to form a sort
of sample, since we were no longer alive.

the sentence has been carried out. the incubation,
staged. to call on outer fringes, to sort or brace
our finds. the night-nurses pressed together while
we boxed up rubber bands. drove this way
through naked vistas, still unbroken from the fog.

DUSTAN

without a moment of transition – as far back as we remember –
in the manner of the system – the moon assumed its place

not entirely black – the rag against our shoulders – from the
concrete walls of silica – the cats were howling in

in the manner of the system – as far back as we remember – in
a spirit once roguish – we shoveled through the sand

now resting on our elbows – as far back as we remember – the
frame was topped with basins – not entirely black

in the manner of the system – there were some who dropped in
shadow – as far back as we remember – before and after dusk

five floors beneath the pantry – hanging up to cure the flowers
– in the manner of the system – the cats were howling in

without a moment of transition – in a spirit once roguish – the
rag against our shoulders – suggested something would begin

as far back as we remember – five floors beneath the pantry –
now resting on our elbows – before and after dusk

SIST .OI

among the creatures of our witnessing

these had vomited up their milk

grown in tight   little ruminants

yet abandoned
from the cheek

the heads of the sisters

above all else they were
the heads of the sisters

one isolated shot skid past our wild home

but no matter :
come to raptor   in fashion

we will meet in hot cartilage
round for sight in prone position :
one great salvo suit

among the creatures of our witnessing
with great hopes of hot cartilage
to above all else our movements

these adapted to our movements
in their slow march to
the ground

PARADES

|^<:>^|

|^<:>^||^<:>^|

angolips, we lash ourselves and back : the
morning bones. no deep sore was it so-
so to give up in narodé. they stay?
switch odiloff the tune. we taglano
forget and go inflex : what slips the room.

|^<:>^|

upland was it or scattered so the fist?
our foreign sines. finger, farro. spittor
in stone. the switch that rolconides.
gallé-gallé! this tender lisp, was that they
stay they stayed. and outers on,
tibilacon : not one but eight? parades.

|^<:>^||^<:>^|

|^<:>^|

|^<:>^|

even cranes have isolation, "seek the
coop" in tender ways. no it's not so
very raven, such thin walled bones, I'd
say. "I been had polo" sorrows, when
the buildings sighed with feet.
grosbeaks and towhees [is it] goodbye
strangers, "hello meat."

the evening is coming off. −−−−−− dilabè [they gesture], in time to
dailoft. events that keep repeating. −−−−−−−−−−−− tag "hila," hoten.
but eventually, the children. −−−− blur no vibe : −−−−−−− "try them."

in tremble "the strident" rings deep
for the phone. a grand space for
feasting, such rare [delicious cold].
yet in that "substance" moment,
trampled voices of the known. accept
this endless fever [and get going] for
the gone.

it's just no good, this knot. −−− irriga, the empties, "a tip for the top."
they know not what they're doing. −−−−−−− in simpla : "better use."
note all the missing trust. −−−−−−− scope lato regions [finga], or go
"dusting for your dust."

ON THE MOVE

a battery for its life, a glow so novel
in its mechanics – what that the waves
wouldn't smash : its inner compass –

would rack into the crumbling
yard : tear off matter, go terra,
stratta, in water it goes slack

or round to wonder, in any case, on the move
once more it is on the move. with four cases
of stark, its wakefulness stilling, and sandy in its stride

still Slater-sandy, if you don't mind, now flicker up
to channel five? it is oily in its nature, this orm-filled
bright occasion, the lighted pieces fall

but nothings wasted :

we are moving on
from one to ones.

MACHINES ON THE MOVE

these carousels are natural, though they work against
our nature. even sleepsprawl lies the willowed
word to sharpen, to :
a power in its shape.

when one saw the yellow – false ridges of
the Spalicht – when the swing of the beams
        kept them under control.

the Sawyer gadgets here were lesser :
were they each the lesser monster. were they no
but they were friendlies at the every morning chopping.
chopping each and every ground.

OTOZO

(* ~ *)
" "

fact is, we had speedlore : broke through dense ooga-lain. passed
through landmarks and *globots* [just the club pools remain]. years of
the cold haunch slashed to half for our grain. half gone with the *titlor*,
half froze just the same.

no mask lomit eagle, skarp over, sig-off. go *staachi* for liver,
every lick to the top. to the lopane, exuber! nitozo, hulcon.
no indolborg, spor-spor.
the *otozo* has come.

trustworthy liquids hold their *bilicol* tongues. and the enzos that rule drift
otozo along. the passageway *blotips* stood through deep *horti-son*. what
space closed off sequence, breaks in feverish charm.

no troves of the basko can orbit the loft.
no bergolen staachi, rare meat that was sought. nitozo,
das plungar! vos regel, vultron. indurt to la slobics!
the *otozo* has gone.

what *sendars* these thumplings what
gunlors what slate had the ice *enzos*
moaned out of cannibal pate just to
bury Otozo? in networks what
grate pounding no thankful *indlor*
sends these harrows. it is late.

oh really cause, the hens —————— and still, the limp that were
these hands. so often it was the case. ———— quick rinse in time
seed slow until ————————————————————– the dog
it barked for noon. ———————————— precious little airs.
—————————————— we vanish in legs to the eleventh floor.
————————————————————————————————
————————————————————————————————

they never came, the rest that were these kind. ————————— so
often it was the case. ——— this way through panes, the second
————————————————————————————————lock.
————————————————————————————————
————————————————————————————————

imagine that we move. ————————————————————
talk up the walls, spread rain into ———————————— the roof
a silent spin. ———————————————— for rocks that
drift what graceless wings no —————————— quieter than
before. passed nights alone, broke fresh indoors so often ————————
—— the case for the wind. ————————————————————
————————————————————————————————
————————————————————————————————

prowlers stood through the light ——————————————————
of it all. the rain fell back ——————————— to the room.
dark after. ————————————————————————————
it's noon. —————————————— these puffs that fall for sleep.

ACKNOWLEGDMENTS

Grateful acknowledgment is made to the editors of the following journals, where some of these poems first appeared: *The Claudius App, CutBank, Lana Turner, petri press, Super Arrow,* and *Wag's Revue.*

Many thanks also to Cal Bedient, Gillian Conoley, Jim Galvin, Doug Powell, Cole Swensen, Jon Thirkield, and Elizabeth Robinson for their support. Special thanks to Peter Burghardt for the thoughtful book design, and to Boodle, for everything.

Sara Deniz Akant received a BA from Wesleyan and an MFA from the Iowa Writers' Workshop. Her work has appeared in *The Claudius App, jubilat,* and *Lana Turner.* She received the John Logan Prize and awards from the Academy of American Poets, the James Merrill House, and Yaddo. She was born and raised in New York.